Magic for Business

Rafe Nauen

©2018

Contents

Contents 2
Copyright Notice 3
Acknowledgements 3
Contact 3
Introduction 4
Animism and Shamanism 6
Ideas about Magic 9
    The Black Candle. 9
    The Board Room Portrait 10
    Principles about Power Animals 12
Power Animals in Business 14
    General 14
    Ant 14
    Badger 15
    Bear 16
    Crocodile or Alligator 16
    Crow 17
    Donkey 17
    Eagle 18
    Elephant 19
    Fox 19
    Giraffe 19
    Gorilla 20
    Hawk 21
    Monkey 21
    Mouse 22
    Snake 23
    Swan 23
Magical Protection 25
    Burglar alarm 25
    Barbed wire 26
    Being somewhere else 26
Constellations 27
Other tools 28
    Problem Identification Game 28
    Tarot Cards 28
    Letters 29
    Job Interviews? 30
    Setting Intentions 30
    Metaphors 31
Function of Magic in Business 32

Copyright Notice

All rights reserved. This book or any portion thereof
may not be reproduced or used in any manner whatsoever
without the express written permission of the publisher
except for the use of brief quotations in a book review.
Printed in the United Kingdom
First Printing, 2018
ISBN-13: 978-1718938656
ISBN-10: 1718938659

Published by Rafe Nauen using CreateSpace.com – an Amazon Company
The book is identified as the sole work of Rafe Nauen ©2018

Acknowledgements

Along the way, many things have contributed to my own understanding of magic in business. The Thursday group – Julie, Lou, Sarah and Andrea. To DHA – a testbed of some extraordinary magic. To my family who introduced me to magic in the first place – how can you have children and not acknowledge magic. Books like Animal Spirit Guides by Stephen Farmer, Acknowledging What Is by Bert Hellinger and the process of learning constellations through training with thecsc.net and experience running workshops – to all my clients – thank you.

Contact

rafe@rafenauen.com +44 7889 523164
www.rafenauen.com www.rafesworkshops.com

Introduction

What is magic, and how can it help in any part of life? Surely business is just business!

Well, how wrong would you be. Would you go for a bank loan on Friday the 13th, or Thursday the 12th out of choice? And if you did, might you blame the 13th as the reason you failed?

And before you set off for that business meeting, you'd prepare right? – learn about your business and the other party, and perhaps about yourself. So, what about mindfulness, calmness, health, etc? "Of course," I hear you say?

Well, in the following pages you'll find a host of tools to augment your position for these and many other events. When the kids are shouting, do you shout back, or go quiet, or coldly punish. All these things are tools for managing other people to best effect. Definitely for you, and potentially for the other party too. When you convey calmness to your kids in a difficult scenario, you benefit, but so do they. This what this book is about.

So, you will find in this book some odd things, some weird things, but always it is designed to help you have better information for good business decisions, and to appreciate any undercurrents you might need to negotiate. Just as someone rowing the Atlantic would need a map of currents and tides (the hidden dynamics of the journey) as well as a compass and map for the route, and likely destination point, so too do we all need a map. This book is a map of some of the hidden dynamics you might encounter on any journey.

So, whats the key?

To my mind, remaining open to all opportunities as a starting point, and recognise that everything has a story or a contribution.

For example, like many of my generation, my father was a man who had been through a war and wanted the very best for his kids. That meant working hard and striving to do the best we could – at all times, and in all places. However, it also meant a paralysis was available, as the possibility of success, and the sought-after reward for success became ever further out of reach. For some this was debilitating and restrictive. For me, magic came early, and never left, so I thought – "what's the point in trying?" Well before Yoda, I thought, "Do, or not do, there is no try!" Because with my father's philosophy to guide me, **trying** always resulted in failure to succeed.

So, read all the information – and I am not talking notes, essays and theses – I am talking everything. If you always make bad decisions on a Friday, don't make ANY decisions on a Friday. If wearing a red skirt, or tie always seems to get you a better deal, then wear a red skirt or tie that day.

The book here is designed to add to that list and encourage a freedom with the magic of the universe to help you make the very best of everything. I have concentrated on business here, mainly because I firmly believe it should be in all contexts of life, and the most unlikely is what appears to be the dry and dusty world of business.

It's not new this idea! The Bank of England has railings with symbols embedded to reinforce the idea of protection:

And you will find in Nottingham a considerable number of statues of dragons:

Why? Well dragons are fearless, burn off first attacks and can fly over things and see for themselves – and make decisions with utter confidence. Why not have that energy within a city. Now the consequences could be more fire power in Nottingham – it is gun capital of UK outside London so who knows? Maybe it has back fired! (just food for thought as you read this little book)

Animism and Shamanism

There is much talk these days of shamanism and less so of animism.

What are they?

A shaman, literally, is a special type of person from Outer Mongolia or Siberia who was by generations of training able to shift energy to such an extent that they could fly, change into animals and so on. The word has become associated with many peoples across the world, and there are plenty of charlatans who get quite a bit of money and power from offering shamanic courses and assistance to clients.

From Wikipedia ***Animism*** *(from **Latin** anima, "**breath**, **spirit**, **life**")*[1][2] *is the **religious belief** that objects, places and creatures all possess a distinct spiritual essence.*[3][4][5][6] *Potentially, animism perceives all things—animals, plants, rocks, rivers, weather systems, human handiwork and perhaps even words—as animated and alive. Animism is the world's oldest religion, "Animism predates any form of organized religion and is said to contain the oldest spiritual and supernatural perspective in the world. It dates back to the Palaeolithic Age, to a time when... humans roamed the plains hunting and gathering and communing with the Spirit of Nature."*[7]

This aspect is easier to be clear about what we mean. It involves being totally aware of the ecology of every situation. To the simple mind I get on a bus with my bus pass to go to town, and it costs nothing because I have a bus pass.
To the animistic mind the bus pass is an honour bestowed on elderly people or disabled people and it is a way of distributing wealth from the young to the old, and it enables bus companies to remain popular and reduce reliance on personal forms of transport. And so on. There is no end to the ramifications of that mind, because there will always be a follow on to the last bit.

So, I hear you say, is that what I really want? Especially in business "Get in quick, do the deal, and get out!"
Well, How about this scenario.

I want to buy a second-hand car. In a hurry. I check my budget, I look up reviews of old cars and I know what sort of car – diesel, estate, toward etc. But at the end of that process the most important factor is the seller. Do I trust him or her?

The trick with magic is to go behind the known ideas and enter the spirit realm in order to get MORE information. Never use that as the only information. So perhaps as you go to bed and think about sleep, ask for a dream to help get you the best car. In the morning you wake and see yourself smiling and shaking the sellers hand with the car you looked at. Perfect. Or you wake and see the car in a ditch.

These are animistic tools. You are concentrating your energy on the entire ecology of a project rather than the direct thought invoked knowledge.

Drums, rattles, music and other things that can get you into a semi trance state will help you to access the truth of things without the noise of the logic in your brain.

Ideas about Magic

By magic I am referring to non-science – to the idea that something other exists and that you may be able to get help from it.

This book is designed to stimulate your own ideas, not be a prescriptive list of things you need to do. Its designed to help you get more outside your brain and thinking, not add to the overload you already have with yet another layer of information that you would need to assimilate. This book is a list of ideas to get you thinking about the ideas that come from you, not from me.

They are all things I have used myself, sometimes often, and often frequently.

The Black Candle.

Using a sharp needle, scratch down the length off a black candle the name of someone you need to feel less conscious or intimidated by – perhaps your ex husband or wife, or a business partner that embezzled a lot of money and then disappeared. You get the idea.

Light the candle in a special place and allow yourself time. Watch for a while as the candle burns down – if you can for its whole journey. At the end you will feel less anxious, more empowered, less bounced by the outer and stronger in the inner.

How, and why?

You have allowed yourself into a realm where science has no place (yet? perhaps?) you have acknowledged that there is more than information available, and especially the limited information you personally have possession of. You have acknowledged another world in which wordless communication has taken place. You have told the universe that you need less of the influence of the name on the side of the candle, and in response the candle has burnt down in honour of that process.

I use the black candle a lot. It allows me peace of mind and reduces the influence in my mind of things that belong in the past that I never had any control of, but if I allow them, could become a serious disturbance to my present, without any possibility of shifting the issue. I might not sleep as well, eat as well or work as I do, and the outcomes of all my business and pleasure experiences could be inferior without the simple tool of a black candle which I sometimes use! Remarkable.

The Board Room Portrait

Why do old board rooms often have a portrait of the founder? Often expensively painted by a famous artist. Why?

Honour – that's all. But what is the effect?

In a modern world many of these things get ignored, at our peril. The board that fails to recognise its roots in that way, may well find itself with a board member who behaves as though they ARE the founder. And with the same attitudes and issues about change in this fast-moving world. The consequence is that that board members resistance may hold up plans and delay emerging futures to the detriment of the business. It's as though in any business, the founder matters as an energy. Nobody has confirmed it scientifically, but everyone can think of examples without too much trouble.

Take Bill Gates. He made a fortune with Microsoft and left in 2014 – but his name is still synonymous with Microsoft. It would be equally ludicrous not to honour Steve Jobs' part in Apple. But lesser organisations forget this.

Is it magic? Yes absolutely. Why? Because of the lack of science. The lack of clear a+b = c access to the whys and wherefores. There is absolutely no technical connection between the hanging of a picture of a man who died 150 years ago with the confidence of the board members of today. But there is an observed connection, and low-cost solutions that seem to have a big effect, are perfectly useful in my book! That a business will go better if you hold a Founder's Day, could seem ridiculous, until you realise that the Founder's Day honours your roots – so everyone feels a little more connected, important, safe, relaxed, healthy – and so on. WOW – can I really attribute all that to such a simple fact? Well, yes actually I can and do!! Many people go through life struggling with their feeling of belonging – family, workgroup, friendship groups, even marriage with in-laws. So, anything that assists that will have a knock-on effect of stimulating change, growth, and feeling of belonging.

Principles about Power Animals

What is a power animal, and what is it not!

A power animal is an idea of an animal that brings a needed aspect to a situation.

An example: In 2013 I became chair of a charity DHA (dhadvice.org) a business that helps people with advice on housing. It gets funding from the legal aid agency but provides the advice from qualified solicitors for free. The charity has two properties – one in Derby, one in Ilkeston that are owned by DHA but mortgaged heavily to RBS. In 2008 they shifted the agreement to 2% over base rate from 1% over base without reference and added in a kind of PPI insurance called an Interest Rate Hedging Product (IRHP). In 2013 the monthly premiums (because the interest rate had gone DOWN) were jeopardising the business, and RBS were preparing to foreclose.

They installed a business advisor at £1000 per 2-day month to increase the burden on us. We fought. BBC Radio Derby interviewed me, and we ended up in Parliament with our MP, Chris Williamson, our RBS Bank Relationship Manager, three from the RBS Remediation team, our CEO and me for a meeting. On the way there by an underground escalator I saw a picture of a gorilla. Probably advertising London Zoo. I thought little about it.

Towards the end of the meeting where we had shown the paper trail proving that they had lied and were clearly on the wrong foot, the Head of Remediation announced that we needed to negotiate an outcome.

It was then that gorilla joined in. I actually had my knuckles on the desk as I rose a little and stated (yes, stated) that
   a. we were here to get our money back
   b. we needed it all
   c. we needed it within 7 days

d. the consequences of non-action on their part was court action where would cite their admission of culpability witnessed in parliament.

We got £516,000 within the seven days by BACS

You can be a cynic and note that nothing came from the gorilla. But what if the animal I had seen was a snake, or a kitten, or an eagle? Immediately, anyone reading this book at this moment will realise the different outcomes and hence the influences of different animal spirits – in business.

Power Animals in Business

General

The idea is that whatever shows up will lead you to a better understanding of your situation and enable a greater chance of making better decisions than without. The list is not definitive or in order of importance to you, and you are completely at liberty to modify, adapt or disagree with the aspects I suggest. The point is that the metaphor that animals will evoke have a place in helping you understand the hidden dynamics within any given situation. Nor are they restricted to business deals. They apply to any situation where knowing a little more, getting a sign about how to proceed, will help you make better choices and avoid bad ones.

Ant

Ants beaver away on a mission, getting what needs to be done, done without question. So, you notice a stream of ants on your way to a meeting, what do you infer? Lots of work to be done, but all doable in small chunks. You are going to need teamwork to get the task ahead underway and completed. So, questions to ask – is my team up to the job? If yes, great, if no, then work to be done, or the project is not viable. So, a very useful input to the mind work involved in decisions.

Badger

Badgers are Britain's fiercest animal (until Wolves return!) and if you've found a badger in the mix of information about a project, dig in! Stick to your guns. If you have made an offer – stick with that offer no matter and be persistent. Take a look at bear too, as they have many complementary aspects – they hide in caves over winter, are ferocious when challenged and hibernate.

Bear

Think about it. A bear chooses its territory accurately and carefully and polices it with vigour. If your given bear to help you make decisions you need (as with badger) to let go of all compromise. Do what you say you are going to do, and stick with the original boundaries, and trust. A bear chooses a cave, delivers its cubs within, whilst hibernating, and trusts that past decisions were perfectly good enough to allow them all to sleep peacefully, and more importantly wake in the spring with enough energy to find food. Lots and lots of trust.

So, it doesn't mean don't do the deal, you just allow yourself some extra information that may help with the decision-making process.

Crocodile or Alligator

Time to be very protective of your rights, but also a crocodile takes a long time digesting stuff, so if you've seen the image of a croc, then take your time. Make sure you know all you need to know before you act.

Crow

Crows are an extraordinary bird. Very community orientated, very vocal, and they have a very sophisticated hierarchical structure. They have courts and parliaments and indiscretions in the community (stealing an egg for example) can result in a court hearing and expulsion from the community for a period of time, or even for ever.

So how do you interpret events should a crow happen to make its presence felt? The major element is justice, and indeed, speaking up for justice.

Donkey

Slow and sure – however long it takes – take care, be cautious and use your intuition stubbornly with the direction of travel. A donkey can carry an enormous load, so be prepared to experience being very nearly overloaded as the project gets under way, but you need never give up, you'll manage.

Eagle

Eagles can see for miles. They can spot prey at great distance, because they notice disturbance.

You see eagle in some form or another – maybe a company logo, maybe a newspaper article, maybe a whistle brings you an image of an eagle. Who knows, except that now you have a presence of an eagle in your information mix.

Take a long view. Sounds good now, but in five years? *"You say you are continuing but as a sleeping partner. How can I be sure that you won't want to change that later on, say in 3 years?"* Those questions become available. And are augmented by the presence of eagle in your mind.

Elephant

Elephants are all about community and strength. Elephants care for each other and are one of the few species of animal (including humans) that have "aunties". They share other attributes with humans – for example, their love of beer! (Indian houses have been demolished by an elephant that smelled beer!) They are difficult to stop and hard to control, until they learn what is in their best interests. They learn quicker and remember stuff too. So, what do you learn from an elephant showing up? Think about family. What is the deal, meeting, move going to affect? How can you help community in your dealings? It also might be about pushing through something – nothing stops an elephant!!

Fox

If fox shows up, then allow mistrust to become available. Someone is out to trick you. Don't believe anything without questioning the ecology. *"If it sounds too good to be true, it probably is!"* We have all been caught out by the trickster. Allow your imagination to let you see things – it may be that on that journey to an early morning meeting you see a fox – but it may be like with my poster of a gorilla. (Unlikely to actually see a gorilla in town!)

Giraffe

Giraffes are well known for eating food that others can't get to, and you might want to think about obvious metaphors such as what you are about to embark on might be a bit of a stretch

Gorilla

Strength, resilience, standing firm. Easy archetype to understand. Clearly in my previous example there was no way I could even begin to *negotiate* when gorilla was around. You don't negotiate with a silverback, you do what he says. And that was just such a moment in October 2014 in a committee room in Portcullis House, UK Parliament building. I can honestly say that gorilla saved us £100,000 that day. In my normal pleasant, cooperative mode, had the boss of RBS remediation offered £400,000 in a cheque, there and then, I would have agreed. As it was, with that gorilla mentality pervading my subconscious mind, 5p short of the figure we had arrived at would have been an insult to our integrity, and only £516,000 would do. And that's what we got. 100% - in full and final settlement.

Hawk

Kestrel, sparrow hawk, buzzard. They remain incredibly alert, can twist in turn in the air, and can hover, awaiting the right moment to act to ensure success. So, when such a creature shows up, pay attention. Be ready to act, and act quickly and decisively having every confidence in all your faculties or alternatively to abandon the project altogether with the same degree of confidence. You will notice that a bird of this sort never sulks, never abandons hope. They just resume ultimate readiness and alertness for the next opportunity, and this is the lesson that Hawk brings you in all your dealings

Monkey

Monkeys are very adaptable, can change direction left or right, and up or down very quickly without missing a beat. If you are looking at monkey in the mix, then you'll find that things are as they are, and that it is you who needs to do the adapting.

Mouse

There is no danger that the mouse will ever become extinct, despite being on the menu of an incredible number of animals. It's prolific and if you watch a mouse its whiskers never stop moving. It is incredibly sensitive to vibration and sound, so is constantly examining the environment for unforeseen dangers. There is no point in a mouse getting angry or despairing if its babies get eaten. If all the mice that had ever been born had lived to old age, then we would live on a planet, three feet deep in mice! So, it manages its expectations.

Mice can get pregnant at 4 weeks old, have four litters in a year, and have up to 12 each time. The first babies can be pregnant at 4 weeks and so on. So, a mouse expects to lose to predation about 95% of its own progeny (if all mice survived it runs into billions in the first year)

Mouse has shown up, what do you do, or think?
Well, you need to stop thinking looking and listening, and start to feel. To be sensitive. You are buying a property and the vendor has three people who have offered when mouse shows up. Well, it might mean that the vendor is not going to go on "no chain" or price, or speed, but how sensitive you are to what you plan to do with the property, so although you make the highest bid, you don't get the property because the vendor feels that you will tear down all their good ideas for the property immediately you move.

So, you understand that you need to be sensitive. You talk about what they did, and why. You ask about family, and history etc. And then you find your offer, although the lowest, has been accepted. Mouse!

Snake

Snakes often hide, disappear, pretend to be sticks, can bite, can constrict, and metaphorically seem to be connected with betrayal – *"You utter snake, you"*

So now you are about to embark on a major business transaction and a snake has turned up in your mind somehow. What to do? Well, all the above or at least some aspects might apply, and the interference of snake will have alerted you to your intuitive mind of the pitfalls in this transaction. Once again, they seldom if ever give an immediate veto. It's just that now you are better equipped to make good decisions and choices – better informed.

Swan

The stereotype of a swan is smooth gliding on the surface, lots of panicky movement underneath. So, if you find yourself thinking about swan, you might consider that the project has a lot of unseen activity to explain its serene exterior appearance. That could be a warning, or an explanation of an otherwise unseen contradiction. You are house-hunting and find the perfect property in the perfect location buts its £100,000 cheaper than you expected.

The lake outside gets your attention and for some reason the swan catches your eye. Dig deeper. Find out what the activity beneath the surface is telling you. Maybe it's not as sinister as the whole project is a money laundering scam, but you might find the next plot has been sold rather expensively and you suspect buildings that would devalue the property in your purview. And no planning permission yet so a quick sale is necessary.

Magical Protection

With any magical work you need some protections – otherwise you'll go mad. Not every animal you see is a power tool for your next adventure. Not every cloud that looks like doom is foretelling your imminent death, so you need some scoping measures.

Surprisingly perhaps, but we have tools within to check the validity of everything. And the most useful (I find) is that if you just say (perhaps sotto voce) *"is this true"* there seems to be an answer. "YES" generally feels stronger, more upright, happier, warmer, and "NO" seems to lower the shoulders, feels cooler, less important.

Always remember that the truth is simply the truth, whereas something other than the truth has to be made up on the spot or remembered or adapted. Watch for those signs too, but it shows why checking like I suggest might indeed yield an answer.

There are other tools to protect you from yourself and the magic

Burglar alarm

Find a thing in your home or office that generally points one way, or maybe a picture that periodically you seem to need to straighten. The next time you need to straighten it, recognise that you just need to check yourself. Is there a business deal that needs attention, a bank that needs a phone call, or does your spouse need a theatre trip because you've been working really hard, and neglecting something? This is your burglar alarm. Warning you that something in your life needs attention. Ignore at your peril. It's a brilliant and simple tool for easier living.

Barbed wire

Barbed wire keeps stuff out. So, develop a technique for perhaps leaving work at work, or not taking calls after 7.30 or whatever you decide. Reinforced boundaries to the elements of your life so that you can simply and easily manage your life work balance better and be protected from the things that interfere with that.

Being somewhere else

Listen to that inner voice that we all have. Without going crazy, be aware that we know stuff, without necessarily knowing how we know stuff. Listening to that can enable you to be somewhere else when bad things happen. Sounds dramatic, and of course if it's that inner voice that stops someone getting onto a doomed plane, then yes of course, but often it is in a much simpler range of experience.

Business meeting versus kid's soccer match choices. You need to be at one, and you choose. If you get into business magic, then that's the moment when you do the right thing. So, you decide the soccer wins. You phone your line manager and tell him you won't be at the meeting because your daughter needs you at the game, but feel they know your position, and can proceed without you. He accepts it, feels honoured with the simple truth, and is envious of your clarity. (that's not the absolute certain outcome by the way, but you get the point)

Constellations

Constellations are a bit weird. Not strictly magic, but then what is? Constellations are about mapping the elements of a system that appear when you ask that system to reveal itself. The map then helps the individual to become acutely aware of the part he or she plays in the bigger picture of their life, work, or simple journey.

One person in a team will chose people to represent different people or aspects within the system in question. The representatives will reveal what it feels like to be in that place, which will be different to their own thoughts – it's as though the system is revealing its own hidden dynamics for the good of the system. For example, someone may find themselves representing a person much higher up in the organisational structure than he or she. Suddenly they have an insight into the pressures and responsibilities of that "place". The exercise can be done with a whole team or with individuals, but it is better to employ the services of a trained facilitator as they can help get some revealing dialogues going. The outcome of such an exercise is that people in the team will understand their place in the hierarchy much better, and therefore be more settled, balanced and indeed happy.

Why in this book about magic? Because it would be very hard to explain exactly what has gone on in the process directly. No-one got a pay rise (some may realise they're in the wrong job though!!) and it is that aspect that this book is all about – taking the dryness out of normal business by engaging with other universal experiences to engage the world of work with all the other worlds. The outcomes of these processes are always positive, because the worst-case scenario is always the status quo. It always augments the experience.

Other tools

Problem Identification Game

Your making business decisions and you feel the need to expand the thinking – it feels like you're missing something. We've all been there. Or it's a brand-new project and we need to brainstorm. The game is this. Get the team together. Take a dictionary and ask three people to choose a number – one between 1 and 300, one between 1 and 9 and the third between 1 and 9. The first is the page number, the second the number of the word on that page, the third is a word that you need to pair with the title of the project.

Turn on the radio and the first big word gets the same treatment. And I feel certain that you will come up with other ideas of problem pairs.

Why? Because it forces you out of tramlined thinking, and into new avenues where onlookers will see the breadth of vision.

Tarot Cards

Yes, I am serious. What they do is force a separation of the elements of a project, an individual or an idea into its elemental parts so that you can review. Don't expect a gypsy woman with a crystal ball, just all the process to shift the thinking into wider contexts. You can use playing cards just as easily as any others, and they still work

The top card – the significator represents the place you are in and will demonstrate a weakness or a strength to you.

What's in the atmosphere, or the environment show if there's trouble ahead or smooth sailing. Elements coming in or going out shows you what you have dealt with already, and stuff you need to be aware will be around. Take a good look at the cards, and just interpret them for yourself. What's in the cross current? What's at the root of it all?

All these questions get answered not because the cards have inherent magical power, but because you have asked to be shown some simple alignments of feeling and asked for a map. Those cards are the answer to that questioning. And they access your hidden memories and subconscious mind and lay it out succinctly before you.

Letters

Did you know you can write a letter, burn it and it have a more useful outcome than if you sent it? Well it's true. The point is you have assimilated your thoughts into a coherent logic and laid them out. So, it has the function outside the etheric to assemble your thoughts. Burn it so you don't dwell on outcomes

Taking it a stage further, you have a relationship with say, your boss that leaves a bit to be desired! You don't want to jeopardise your job, but you need things to change.

Write a letter to him polite but firm about what you see, or feel is wrong with the way he or she acts.

Burn it

Write a reply from the boss that answers the disquiet.

Burn that one too

Write a third letter to your boss – you will notice that everything has changed.

Burn that one too and allow the new conditions of your relationship to apply henceforth.

Job Interviews?

Really want that job?

Write a letter of acceptance to yourself signed by the interviewer – gets you out of a sabotage habit where your "I'll never get that job" interfere with the actual interview! By the time you get to the interview, its already your job!

Setting Intentions

Remove all electronic devices and get comfortable.

Relax

1. Get into a meditative state and clearly set out in your minds eye exactly what you wish

Go to bed, to sleep and when you wake you will be a step closer to that concept you laid out

May be that's not your scene.

2. Put up a vision board
3. Write your intentions for an outcome to a situation or decision. Burn it

All these ideas will help you get nearer achieving your intentions, whatever they are, and however you achieve it. Scientifically its going to enable you to focus on the important elements and forget the padding.

Metaphors

Use metaphors to undermine the spin of any situation and to allow a long view.

If you find yourself cynically objectifying scenarios, don't dismiss the metaphor but instead weave it into your current understanding so that it enhances it, and enables as ever, to make better business decisions.

Function of Magic in Business

As has been alluded to along the journey of this book, the whole idea is to expand thinking, and reduce tramlines.

There's an old phrase "if you always do what you always did, you'll always have what you always had!" in other words, changing thinking patterns is essential for growth and development. New projects need new thinking, and this book is all about shifting thinking patterns, whether by playing a PIG (Problem Identification Game) or noticing the appearance of an animal or running a constellation. There are unlimited tools out there to help us in everyday life. We feel better when the sun is shining and more positive. The term lunatic refers to the phases of the moon – and anyone working in an institution will regard as absolute fact that they have much more daft behaviours during a full moon than at other phases. I suppose there are scientific explanations, but I haven't heard a good one yet! – we are 90% water and the moon has a pull on water on the planet etc. What do you think?

YOU are the key, not me and not the process you chose. This book, as previously stated, is to help you get under the blur of information overload and to access the subconscious which performs an essential but often forgotten part of everyday life.

Listen o the beat of your drum

www.ingramcontent.com/pod-product-compliance
Lightning Source LLC
Chambersburg PA
CBHW031517210526
45464CB00007B/2947